CHRISTMAS at the STABLE

The Animals Tell Their Stories

By Kimberly K. Funk
Illustrated by Kimberly Rempel

Based on an old Christmas carol, *The Friendly Beasts*

Christmas at The Stable–The Animals Tell Their Stories

Published by SEWright Stories 

Edited by June Galle Krehbiel

Special thanks to Laurie Oswald Robinson, Tales of the Times LLC

Cover design, book design and layout by Jim L. Friesen

Library of Congress Control Number: 2016948878

International Standard Book Number: 978-0-9977952-0-2

Printed in the United States of America by Mennonite Press, Inc., Newton, Kansas.
www.MennonitePress.com

For the children of Tabor Mennonite Church, then and now.
And to Darwin and our own children then,
and our grandchildren now.
–K. F.

To Jade, Cole, Riley, and Harry.
Love, laughter, solidarity. Always.
–K. R.

"And she brought forth her firstborn son, and wrapped him
in swaddling clothes, and laid him in a manger;
because there was no room for them in the inn."
–Luke 2:7 KJV

Jesus our brother, kind and good,
Was humbly born in a stable rude,
And the friendly beasts around Him stood,
Jesus our brother, kind and good.

A stable. A little barn. That is where Jesus was born. A barn does not have a bed. A barn does not have heat. A barn does not have a nice floor and walls. A barn has barn smells, and barn noises, and barn straw and barn dirt. It is a barn. Not a house. Not a home for people. It is a home for animals.

That is where Jesus was born. In the home of animals. The animals were there when Jesus was born. After Mary and Joseph, the animals were the first to see Jesus, and to welcome Jesus, and to love Jesus. They have stories to tell. The animals' stories are here for you, dear children, in this book. Listen to the stories they tell.

"I," said the donkey, shaggy and brown,
"I carried his mother up hill and down,
I carried her safely to Bethlehem town,
I," said the donkey, shaggy and brown.

THE DONKEY'S STORY

I am a gentle donkey, and I belong to a man named Joseph. I have lived in Nazareth all my life, and Joseph is always kind to me. He is a carpenter, and I often help him carry supplies and tools that he uses as he works. One day he came to me and seemed a bit troubled.

"Well, my little shaggy friend," he said, "tomorrow we are going on a trip. It isn't one I want to take, but Caesar, our ruler, says we must travel to Bethlehem to pay a tax to him and also to be counted. And you, my little one, you have an important job. You must carry my beloved Mary, who will soon have a baby."

When Joseph said this, I perked up my ears. I remembered carrying Mary to a faraway town once to see her cousin Elizabeth. Mary had been so kind and loving to me. I looked forward to seeing her in the morning. I could hardly wait. But that is one thing I have learned—I must always wait patiently so that I am ready whenever someone needs me.

The morning came, and we left on our journey just as the sun began to peek over the horizon. Mary spoke softly as she patted my neck, "Little fellow, you must carry me and my little one safely to Bethlehem."

I didn't understand, there was only Mary. What little one? But then I listened and I did understand. "Soon my baby will come, little fellow, so carry me gently over the rocky hills to Bethlehem."

This is what I did. On each step I placed my hooves gently. The road was rocky and steep at places. I watched for stones and holes in the road and avoided them so I would not stumble. I tried to stay on the road at all times because wild animals or snakes could be hiding in the rocks and bushes. Sometimes Mary walked, and I waited for her to ride me again, staying near her all the time. Sometimes there were streams and rivers to cross, and I was very careful crossing these because I didn't want my precious friend to get wet and cold. When we stopped for the night, I waited patiently to be fed and watered. Then, when Mary slept near the warm fire, I stood sleeping between her and the darkness where creatures of harm might lurk.

We finally arrived in Bethlehem. The streets were so crowded we could barely move. I tried hard not to bump into people and other animals. I needed to keep Mary safe. Joseph tried and tried to find a place to stay, but all the inns were full. Finally, one innkeeper said we could stay in his stable, and so that is where I took Mary. Joseph helped Mary get off my back, and she sat down in the straw as I stood near her and I waited. I wasn't sure what I waited for, but I felt like something important was happening. Mary had said that soon her baby would be born. Could it be tonight?

I waited and waited deep into the night. Then I heard a baby's cry, and I knew the waiting was over. I timidly walked near to where Mary lay and Joseph stood. There in Mary's arms was the sweet baby Jesus. I loved him at once. The awaited one, Jesus, was here.

"I", said the cow, all white and red,
"I gave him my manger for his bed,
I gave him my hay to pillow his head,
I," said the cow, all white and red.

THE COW'S STORY

I am the cow to whom this stable belongs. During the day I graze in the pastures surrounding it, and at night I come to the stable for shelter. The stable is also where I eat clean, sweet hay from a manger.

I was out in the pasture late one afternoon when all at once, I noticed some commotion on the path leading from the inn to my stable. I wondered what it could be. Just what was going on?

I lumbered down the rocky path of the hill and made my way to the stable. As I got closer, I heard a voice say: "This will do just fine, Mary. See, I will make a bed for you on the nice clean hay."

I was puzzled and a bit perturbed. What business did these people have coming to *my* stable and using *my* hay as if they owned the place?

I quickened my pace, but as I neared the entrance to the stable, I was abruptly halted by a donkey I didn't even know—and standing in *my* doorway!

There wasn't much I could do, so I just stood there looking, chewing my cud, and wondering what this was all about.

Slowly the scene before me unfolded. I decided that I must not be so hasty in judging this situation. These people obviously needed a place to rest, and so I decided to leave them alone. I couldn't get into the stable anyway with that donkey in the way. So, I walked behind the stable where I could see a little through a window and think things over.

I could hear the people talking, and the one called Mary said, "Oh, Joseph, soon our baby will be born. How is it that God's Son is to be born here on a bed of hay? I wonder what meaning this can hold."

When I heard her say this, I stopped chewing my cud and began to think. What had she said? "God's Son?" Did she mean the God of all creatures, the creator of the world? His SON? What indeed, I wondered, was this all about?

I stood quietly, chewing my cud again, thinking and wondering about all that was happening. Nighttime had fallen when suddenly I heard a cry. What made a noise like this? I ran back to the door of the stable (that donkey was now inside) and I went inside also.

There, in Mary's arms, was a baby.

How was it that a baby of a human had come to be born in my stable and that I was present as the miracle unfolded? Was this really God's Son, as Mary had said?

As I stepped closer, I was overcome with joy and a desire to help these people in some way. It occurred to me that the baby should have a place to sleep. I thought of my manger. It would be the right size and the straw was clean and sweet smelling.

With my nose I nudged the straw toward the couple, and Joseph noticed.

"Why, Mary," he said, "I do believe this kind cow would like to share her manger with us. We can use it to cradle our Jesus."

"Our Jesus," he had said. I felt like he was my Jesus too. I realized that I had seen the wonder of the birth of God's own Son, Jesus.

"I," said the dove, from the rafters high,
"Cooed him to sleep, so he would not cry,
We cooed him to sleep, my mate and I,
I," said the dove, from the rafters high.

THE DOVE'S STORY

I am a little dove who lives with my mate in a stable in Bethlehem. From my perch high in the rafters of the stable I can watch many activities as they happen. Sometimes I like to fly to the nearby inn and watch travelers as they come to Bethlehem from the hills of Judea.

One day the streets were so crowded and noisy and there was so much to see that I was all a-twitter, not knowing where to perch in order to get the best view.

As I watched from the roof of the inn, I noticed a disturbance by the front door. I heard a man say: "Please, kind sir, my name is Joseph and this is my wife, Mary, and we have traveled for so long. Our baby is soon to be born. Can't you please find room for us?"

I saw my innkeeper hesitate and finally he said, "All right, follow me to the stable out back. I wish I could give you a better place to rest than this, but I have no choice. It is late in the day and my inn is already overflowing."

People staying in my stable? What was this all about? I flew back to the stable to join my mate who was sitting on our nest in the rafters. I watched carefully as these two came in.

They seemed weary and were dusty from their travel, but I could see kindness and gentleness in their manner. Yet, there was also a sense of urgency about them. I quietly flew from my nest and perched on nearby rafters so I could watch more closely.

"Look at the dove in the rafters, Mary," Joseph said. "It seems to be watching us. Seeing it there reminds me of the story of our ancestor Noah and how the dove gave the sign of dry land after the great flood. Surely this stable is a good and safe place for us to stay, for the dove is a sign of God."

My little bird heart fluttered to be spoken of in such a way.

As Mary looked up at me, I again saw the kindness in her eyes and I was drawn toward this couple. I softly flew down to the top of a gate in the stable.

It was getting late, and Joseph helped Mary lie down in the straw. I watched the long night through, and there, in the stable I call home, I watched the birth of a child.

After Mary wrapped the child and fed him and tried to settle him down, the baby whimpered. I saw how tired Mary was. Was there nothing I could do to help? I began to coo my dove song, and my mate joined in. Ever so softly we cooed, hoping it would still the baby called Jesus. While I watched, I thought I saw him smile as he fell asleep. Only then did Mary close her eyes to sleep as well. At last Joseph sat down at the entrance of the stable, as if to guard the door, and his head nodded in sleep too.

All was quiet and peaceful, and my eyes were heavy from watching so much that day. In the peace of the stable, I closed my eyes and fell asleep.

I had watched, and I had seen, and in my heart I knew that this child, Jesus, was from God.

"I," said the rooster, with the shining eye,
"I crowed the news up to the sky,
When the sun arose, I crowed to the sky,
I," said the rooster, with the shining eye.

THE ROOSTER'S STORY

I am the rooster. I live in the corner of the stable which stands near the inn on the outskirts of Bethlehem. Since it is my good fortune to live at the edge of town, I am usually the first to see the travelers as they make their way to this city. I really don't want to brag, but being the first to notice the comings and goings, I always know when something important or exciting is happening. And it is up to me—yes, it is my duty—with my loud, and I might add, beautiful crow, to announce anything of importance to the entire city.

Now of all the things I have seen happen here in Bethlehem, the event I am about to relate to you is the most exciting of all. Because of it, I will never be quite the same ol' bird I was before.

That day, I sat on the stump of an olive tree near the inn at the edge of town. From there I had the best view to see all that was going on. The town was unusually busy due to some sort of decree issued by an emperor. Late in the day I thought about making my way to the stable to roost for the night. That's when I noticed a man leading a donkey with a young woman riding it. They stood out from the others in the crowd, probably because of how urgently they headed down the street. They came to the inn and knocked on the door, asking for a place to stay. The innkeeper finally led them to the stable—the very one where I was going. I half ran and half flew to reach it before they did.

The events in the stable that night left me awed and amazed. So much happened. First, these people came to stay here. Then, if that weren't enough, a baby was born. Yes, a baby boy. Even more amazing, I learned that he was God's own Son.

I know this to be true, because late in the night, after the baby was here, some shepherds I know came running and praising God. They said a band of angels had appeared to them and told them this was God's Son. God's own Son, come to earth to bring peace and good will to all. Near dawn, the shepherds left the stable, rejoicing and shouting the birth of Jesus Christ.

Then many days later, camels and wise men came. They said a star had led them to Baby Jesus. I saw it all—the birth of a Savior, the joy of the shepherds, the brilliant light of the star, and the gifts of the wise men. I was so amazed I almost burst.

So there I was. The rooster with the loud, and I might add, beautiful crow. Yet, what I had seen was so overwhelming, I didn't know how I could possibly declare it to the world. But I would try. With rejoicing I would crow to all who would hear that Jesus our Savior was born!

To this day, when I crow at break of day and set of sun, I crow with rejoicing. This has become my duty. Instead of crowing because I am important, I crow because I have something important to crow about. I use my loud and beautiful crow—which God gave me—to declare to the world with rejoicing, that Jesus, the Savior, reigns forever.

"I," said the sheep, with the curly horn,
"I gave him my wool for his blanket warm,
He wore my coat on Christmas morn,
I," said the sheep, with the curly horn.

THE SHEEP'S STORY

I am a sheep. I make my home here among the lovely hills of Judea surrounding the town of Bethlehem. I belong to a young shepherd boy named Seth (he calls me Pet) and I like to stay near him and follow him. This is probably because I was born a twin and my mother didn't have enough milk for two lambs, so Seth cared especially for me. We are good friends. Last summer, after shearing time, Seth made my wool into a special blanket which he uses at night as he watches over my flock and me.

It is because I'm always following my young shepherd that I was even there when we found Jesus. Let me go back to the beginning.

It was after dark and my flock of sheep had settled in for night. The shepherds burned a fire to keep wild animals away and to warm themselves, for it was a cold night. I lay near Seth as he softly sang one of David's psalms. I liked it best when he sang the one that begins "The Lord is my Shepherd."

All was peaceful and quiet. Now and then a mother softly called to her lamb. I drifted off to sleep. Then suddenly, a light so bright appeared in the sky that I hid my eyes in Seth's lap. I felt Seth tremble. A voice spoke from the light: "Do not be frightened. I've come with good and joyful news! This news is for everyone. Down in Bethlehem, a baby has been born. This baby is Christ the Lord! You can find the baby wrapped in cloths and lying in a manger."

I realized that this must be an angel of the Shepherd called Lord that David wrote about in the psalm. An angel who came to tell my lowly shepherds and us sheep that God had sent his Son to earth. How amazing that we were chosen to receive this good news! But before I had time to give this much thought, I looked up and saw many angels praising God and singing.

Just as suddenly as the angels had appeared, they were gone. All the shepherds were so excited, speaking at once and saying that they must find this baby. They ran all the way to Bethlehem and naturally, I followed Seth, my young shepherd. Because of the excitement, no one even noticed me. We found the stable at the edge of town with a young couple inside and a baby in the manger, just as the angel had said. My shepherds told them what had happened out in the fields. They didn't seem surprised but said God was working in miraculous ways. We entered the stable, and my shepherds fell to their knees by the manger and peered in to see the Christ child announced by the angels.

I nuzzled close to Seth and peeked into the manger too. There lay Jesus. A sweet, tiny baby. Mary's little lamb—so new and precious and dear. Seth noticed me and said, "Ah, Pet, what about you, following me here? I could have known you would. It's cold out tonight. What do you say, Pet, shall we give the baby Jesus this blanket made from your wool?"

I bleated a soft yes, and Seth took the blanket from around his shoulders and gently tucked it around baby Jesus. It seemed that Jesus turned his head toward me and smiled. As Seth gazed at the baby, he patted my head and said softly, "Behold, the Lamb of God."

So there, on that night in Bethlehem, I, a sheep, who lives in the hills of Judea, saw the Son of God. The Lamb of God. Jesus Christ, the Lord, and Good Shepherd.

"I," said the camel, all yellow and black,
"Over the desert upon my back,
I brought him a gift in the Wise Men's pack,
I," said the camel, all yellow and black.

THE CAMEL'S STORY

A camel. That is who I am. A beast of burden. I serve my masters, carrying their cargo and supplies to the places I am led. I can travel over the hot desert sand without water for days at a time, carrying the heavy load my masters pack on my back. I don't mind because that is who I am: a camel, who is a helper and a servant. The masters I serve are magi or wise men. Some people call these wise men *kings*.

Mine is a simple story. I followed a star and found a King, and when I found him I knelt down and worshiped him.

I see questions in your eyes? Let me tell you more. My magi study the stars. One night a magnificent, brilliant star rose in the eastern sky. Somehow, my magi knew it marked the place where they would find a King. A new kind of King. A King who would serve those he came for. A King who would be the Savior of the world. They wished more than anything else that they could find this King, so that they might worship him.

This is the reason I began a journey I will never forget. I was very excited as we set out. At first it seemed strange to follow a star, even one of such magnificence. We did not know where it would lead or at what time we would arrive at some unknown destination. But when you travel with magi, you do unusual things without asking why. Even so, this was most extraordinary.

For many days we traveled through the desert, the brilliant star always guiding us and showing the way.

At one point on our journey we traveled to Jerusalem. We stopped and asked King Herod if he could tell us where this new King was to be found. He could not, but he wanted us to let him know when we found him so he too could worship the Child.

We set out on our journey again, following the star. My masters, wise men that they are, learned in a dream from God that they should never return to Herod. He was really jealous and would want to harm the new King.

So we traveled on, and the star went before us guiding our way.

At long last the star stood still. It shown brilliantly over the town of Bethlehem, nestled in the hills of Judea.

We followed the bold, single ray of light that marked the path for us. It led us to a stable where we found a child, a mere babe, in a manger. Was this the King we had sought? For this we had journeyed so far, following a star? Yes, to find God's Son—Jesus the Christ. We followed a light in the sky and found the light of the world.

My magi had brought valuable gifts that I so willingly carried in my pack, for that long, long trip. With adoration my magi presented these gifts to the Christ child. Our joy knew no end!

That, dear children, is my story. It really is simple. I, a servant of kings, followed a star and found a King who came to serve. And when I found him, I knelt down and worshiped him.

So every beast, by some good spell,
In the stable dark, was glad to tell,
Of the gift he gave Emmanuel,
The gift he gave Emmanuel.

And so, dear children, the animals have told you their stories. Jesus was born in a stable, a little barn. The animals were there when Jesus was born. All the animals gladly gave what they had, little as it may have seemed at the time, to the Christ child. They didn't give because they were told to give or because they thought they might get something in return. They gave because there was a need to give. They gave out of love and compassion. They gave of themselves and from their hearts.

We too can give to the Christ child today. Give yourself, whatever you may have, and give from your heart. Give your heart to Jesus, the Savior of the world.

AUTHOR'S NOTE

Growing up, I vividly recall the Christmas programs which were presented when I was in grade school. So much anticipation and excitement! We lined up in the hallway and marched into the crowded gymnasium, took our places on the bleachers, and sang the Christmas carols we had been practicing for weeks. One song in particular stood out to me—my favorite, "The Friendly Beasts." Growing up on a farm, I knew animals. To imagine them surrounding the newborn Jesus was not a foreign idea in any way. I could feel the love the animals would have had for that dear infant.

When I was asked to write a series of children's stories for Advent though Epiphany at Tabor Mennonite Church, Newton, Kansas, memories of my childhood and the stories I held dear came back to me. This one was still at the forefront. I decided to use this old Christmas carol and tell the stories about the animals who shared the stable where Jesus was born. That was twenty-four years ago. Since that time on several occasions the stories have been adapted for Christmas programs. I could never quite give them up. So now I offer them to you and your children. I pray that you may find the Christ child in these stories, knowing that all God's creatures belong on this good earth and make God's world complete.

–Kimberly Funk